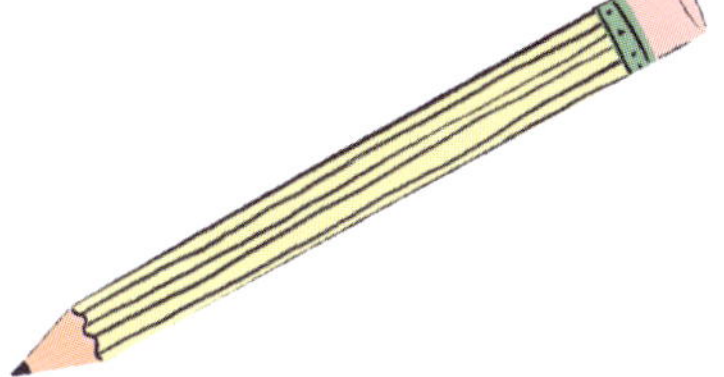

TIME FOR SCHOOL

How Humans Learn

Leah Payne

Illustrated by
Paige Jung

ORCA BOOK PUBLISHERS

Published in Canada and the United States in 2026 by Orca Book Publishers.

Library and Archives Canada Cataloguing in Publication
Title: Time for school : how humans learn / Leah Payne ; illustrated by Paige Jung.
Names: Payne, Leah (Leah S.), author. | Jung, Paige, illustrator.
Series: Orca timeline ; 13.
Description: Series statement: Orca timeline ; 13 | Includes bibliographical references and index.
Identifiers: Canadiana (print) 20250162539 | Canadiana (ebook) 20250163691 |
ISBN 9781459841505 (hardcover) | ISBN 9781459841512 (PDF) | ISBN 9781459841529 (EPUB)
Subjects: LCSH: Learning—Juvenile literature. | LCSH: Education—Juvenile literature. |
LCSH: Schools—Juvenile literature. | LCGFT: Informational works.
Classification: LCC LB1060 .P42 2026 | DDC j370.15/23—dc23

Library of Congress Control Number: 2025932862

Summary: Part of the nonfiction Orca Timeline series for middle-grade readers, this illustrated book examines the past, present and future of schools around the world and the who, what, where, when and how we learn.

Orca Book Publishers is committed to reducing the consumption of nonrenewable resources in the production of our books. We make every effort to use materials that support a sustainable future.

Orca Book Publishers gratefully acknowledges the support for its publishing programs provided by the following agencies: the Government of Canada, the Canada Council for the Arts and the Province of British Columbia through the BC Arts Council and the Book Publishing Tax Credit.

Design by Dahlia Yuen.
Edited by Monique Polak.

Printed and bound in South Korea.

29 28 27 26 • 1 2 3 4

CERTIFIED CANADIAN PUBLISHER

ORCA BOOK PUBLISHERS
orcabook.com

For my teachers.

Thank you for making my school experience so wonderful, showing me the magic of books and encouraging me to keep writing.

Hurry up! School is officially in session.
LUMINOLA/GETTY IMAGES

Contents

PROTECT TRANS KIDS
NO PLANET B
STOP

INTRODUCTION

Do you go to school? If you are reading this book, chances are you do. Maybe you attend an elementary school or a middle school, or maybe you're homeschooled. Maybe you study virtually at a computer or with the help of other forms of technology, or maybe you learn outside in nature. Maybe it's a combination of these options—or even something else entirely!

Humans have always learned, but formal schooling is a relatively recent invention in human history. Why does school exist? Experts have debated the purposes of education for a long time, and they have differing beliefs. Educating young people is important for many reasons. Yes, school teaches us skills so we can have a job one day. In this way, it reduces the chances of poverty. But school also helps us learn about our world, including how to work with others, which values are considered important in our societies and how to improve our communities. In short, school is meant to prepare young people for the world around them.

MASKOT/GETTY IMAGES

Education can be an incredible gift, allowing us to learn fascinating new things, develop important skills and fulfill our dreams for the future. But the history of school hasn't always been rosy. Over the years, school has been dramatically different for children depending on many factors—where they live, how much money their families have and even what they look like. Many people throughout history have not been allowed to attend school—and this remains a huge problem in several places around the world today.

The concept of school is still evolving. During the early days of the pandemic, for example, school shifted online and students learned at home. Today, we continue to ask how schools of the future will adapt with us to reflect our changing world. Experts are examining topics like technology and ***artificial intelligence (AI)***, inclusivity, community involvement and learning in nature.

Looking to the past can give us tools to better understand our present—to help us understand why things are the way they are now. It can also give us ideas of how we would like our future to look. It's important to note that this book takes a mostly Canadian and American perspective. It doesn't cover the entire picture of education, everywhere, throughout time—that wouldn't be able to fit in this book! Rather, I hope to give a glimpse of education in various places and throughout time.

In the following chapters, let's explore the history, present and future of schools: *who* learns, *what* we learn, *where* we learn, *when* we learn and *how* we learn.

The iconic yellow bus as we know it today came about in the 1930s. The bright color was chosen to help increase visibility and safety. Before then, early automobiles and horse-drawn vehicles were sometimes used to help transport rural kids to school.
THOMAS BARWICK/
GETTY IMAGES

c.11,000 BCE
Prehistoric
cave drawing

1831–1996
Residential
schools

1960
Ruby Bridges

1237
Bettisia
Gozzadini

ONE

STUDENTS

WHO GETS TO LEARN?

Doesn't everyone get to go to school? It sure seems that way when you're walking into the building in the morning with all your classmates, everyone jostling at the door with their backpacks, instruments and basketballs. You might be surprised to learn that not everyone gets the opportunity to learn, today and in the past.

Who Attended the First Schools?

Many thousands of years ago, children were taught by their families and community groups. While we might not consider this to be school in the strictest sense of the word, it is education. Our prehistoric ancestors taught their children skills they would need to survive, like how to care for babies and hunt.

However, some children have been denied access to education. We can look to ancient times for examples. In ancient Rome, the wealthiest families often hired tutors so their children could learn at home. Elementary-level education also existed for girls and boys. Ancient Roman schools were not mandatory, and families had to pay ***tuition*** for their children to attend. This meant that many poor children could not attend. Plus, many girls were expected to marry as teenagers and therefore stopped attending school when they were young.

PRESENT
Gender-inclusive bathrooms

JENNER IMAGES/GETTY IMAGES

In one-room schoolhouses, many students of all different ages learned in the same room, and the teacher was responsible for teaching all levels. Often the teacher was a young unmarried woman, who was expected to stop teaching once she married.
WILLIAMSHERMAN/GETTY IMAGES

One-Room Schoolhouses

Around the turn of the 20th century, stricter child labor laws came into effect. These laws meant that more children in the United States and Canada would attend school rather than work.

If you try to imagine an old-fashioned school from around this time, you might envision a one-room schoolhouse with rows of desks. You might have even visited one on a field trip, where you learned how children lived hundreds of years ago. These one-room schoolhouses were common in Canada and the United States in the 1800s and early 1900s.

Although both boys and girls attended school, they were sometimes separated. In a 19th-century schoolhouse, for example, girls and boys might have separate entrances, recess areas and classrooms.

As time went on, basic education became both free and mandatory for children, and different places created and enforced various rules and laws to ensure that children attended school.

Celtic Fosterage

Throughout time, cultures have educated young people in many creative ways. Have you ever wondered what it would be like to grow up in another family? Celtic ***fosterage*** in medieval Ireland and Scotland was the practice of sending children off to live with a neighboring family, who would help raise them and teach them practical skills over several years. Skills were taught according to gender. For example, boys might learn how to herd cattle, and girls might learn how to sew clothes and cook. The practice of fostering didn't just help to educate children—it also helped maintain peace and friendship between different groups of people.

These days, school exchange programs also offer children the chance to temporarily live with another family. Doing so helps children learn about another part of the world, practice speaking another language and make friends abroad. Popular countries for students to visit include France, Germany, Italy, Spain and Japan. Which countries are on your travel bucket list?

MASKOT/GETTY IMAGES

Residential Schools

To say that everyone had equal access to education during this time is false, however. For Indigenous children, the experience was completely different from that of white children of European descent. For thousands of years, Indigenous people had educated their children through ***land-based education*** (see chapter 3). Land-based education, thankfully, still exists today, despite the efforts of the Canadian government to sever Indigenous children from their cultures during the process of ***colonization***. A prime example of colonization is the establishment of residential schools.

First founded in the 1830s, residential schools were religious boarding schools first run by different Christian churches, and then by the government of Canada. These schools removed Indigenous children from their families, with the intention of ***assimilating*** them into European-Canadian and Christian culture. The Canadian government and Christian churches didn't want only to assimilate the children—they also wanted to destroy all forms of Indigenous culture. This practice makes residential schools a method of ***cultural genocide***.

The children were forcibly removed from their communities, taken from their families and required to live at residential schools. They were punished for speaking their languages, practicing their cultural traditions and eating their traditional foods. The education they received was poor. The students were taught to feel shame about their culture and who they were. They were often abused, underfed and malnourished. Many died from abuse or as an indirect result of abuse (such as getting sick due to malnourishment). An estimated 150,000 children attended residential schools in Canada. Residential schools existed in the United States as well.

The last Canadian residential school closed in 1996, which means they operated for more than 160 years. Many residential school Survivors continue to deal with trauma from the abuse they endured. When the Survivors grew up and had children of their own, many were unable to pass along their Traditional Knowledge, language and culture or parent effectively, as they'd been taken away from their own parents. This intergenerational trauma continues to affect Indigenous communities today. It's our responsibility to commit to the goals of ***truth and reconciliation*** as we listen to the stories of residential school survivors and work toward ***decolonization***.

In Canada September 30 is Orange Shirt Day. This annual event honors those who attended residential schools. People wear the color orange, take time to reflect and gather together at various events.

The University of al-Qarawiyyin is still in operation today.
ALEXEY PEVNEV/SHUTTERSTOCK.COM

Off to College

The oldest Western university is considered the University of Bologna, in Italy. It was founded in 1088. However, even older than that is the University of al-Qarawiyyin, in Fez, Morocco. It was first founded as a mosque in 857 to 859, by a Muslim woman named Fatima al-Fihri. It's important to note, though, that universities have historically excluded women, with rare exceptions. Harvard University, for example, did not allow women to study law until 1950, even though women petitioned to be allowed to study at Harvard Law School as far back as 1871.

Bettisia Gozzadini was one of the first women to earn a university degree. She studied law at the University of Bologna and graduated in the year 1237, during the Middle Ages. She later taught law at the University of Bologna. She is believed to be the first woman to teach at a university.

In the year 1920, women made up only 16 percent of ***undergraduate*** students in Canada. In 1986 this number had grown to 50 percent, making the number of female undergraduate students finally equal to the number of male undergraduates.

MILLA1974/GETTY IMAGES
A NEPOTI/WIKIMEDIA COMMONS/PUBLIC DOMAIN

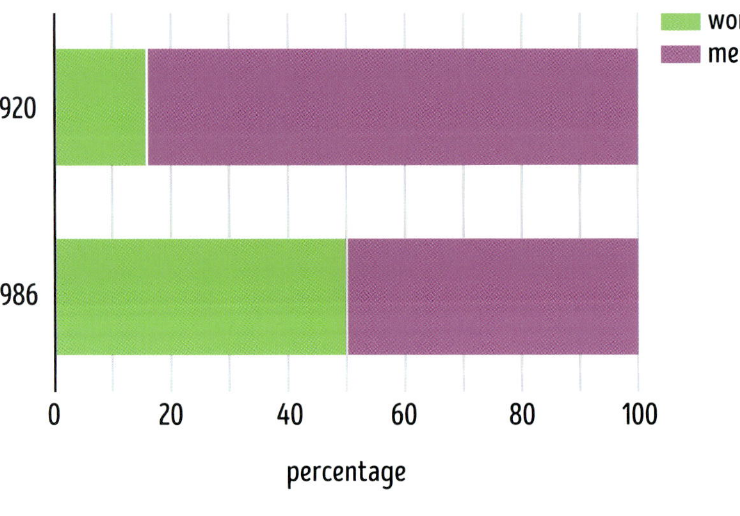

Segregation in Schools

As we can see, education was rarely equally accessible throughout history. In the recent past in both Canada and the United States, students were segregated based on ***race***, meaning they were separated and sent to different schools based on the color of their skin. In the United States, it wasn't until 1954 that this segregation was deemed ***unconstitutional*** in the famous *Brown v. Board of Education* legal case, and Black and white students were officially allowed to attend public school together. However, things didn't change right away in many parts of the country. The *Brown v. Board of Education* decision angered lots of white people. Some of them held protests and enrolled their children in private schools.

In 1960 a brave six-year-old girl named Ruby Bridges became the first Black student to integrate into a public elementary school in the Southern United States. She had to be escorted by police officers to keep her safe as she walked past the angry, screaming crowd of adults on her way to school. Several white parents withdrew their children once they learned Bridges would be attending, leaving her as the only child in her class for the first year. She ate lunch alone and sometimes played with her teacher—a white woman named Barbara Henry. Henry came from Boston to teach Bridges, as the other teachers refused. Bridges graduated from a desegregated school and remains a civil rights ***activist*** to this day.

Canadian public schools were segregated too, in several different ways. For example, in the early and mid-19th century, some areas in Ontario had separate buildings for Black students, or Black students attended a one-room schoolhouse at a different time than white students. Sometimes they attended at the same time but had to sit on different benches. The last segregated school in Ontario closed in 1965. In Nova Scotia, the last segregated school closed in 1983. In some areas of Canada, students were also separated by religion, with Catholic and Protestant students attending different schools.

Asian Canadians have also faced segregation and racism in Canada, such as being placed in separate classes. In British Columbia, the Victoria school board voted to fully segregate Chinese students in 1922. Prior to this time, partial segregation had existed. Thankfully, a students' strike organized by the Chinese Canadian Club, Chinese Consolidated Benevolent Association and the Chinese Commerce Association led the school board to overturn its decision. However, full integration of Chinese students in Victoria schools didn't occur until after World War II.

The Chinese Consolidated Benevolent Association and Chinese Public School is still based in Victoria, BC, today.
MICHAL KLAJBAN/WIKIMEDIA COMMONS/ CC BY-SA 4.0

What Is Intersectionality?

Intersectionality is a term that explains how aspects of our identities, such as ethnicity and gender, interact and create individual experiences of either privilege or oppression. The term was developed by American civil rights advocate, scholar and writer Kimberlé Crenshaw in 1989. Our different identities mean we all see the world in different ways and have unique experiences.

We can use intersectionality as a way to examine and understand many things—including education. For example, a white girl in America in the 1960s would have a different experience of school than a Black girl in America in the 1960s. The white girl would experience sexism due to her gender but would not experience racism due to the color of her skin. The Black girl, on the other hand, would experience both sexism *and* racism.

What are some of your identities? Consider taking a moment to reflect on them and your experiences, and how they shape who you are as a person.
FG TRADE/GETTY IMAGES

Who Attends School Today?

In many places around the world, all children receive education, which is mandated by the area's government. Education is considered a basic ***human right***.

However, although all children should have access to education in *theory*, not all children have access to education in *practice*. Many children around the world are denied education. Poverty as well as conflict and political instability (like war) make it challenging for some children to attend school. Children may not live close enough to a school, they may have too many responsibilities at home to go to school, or they may lack qualified teachers.

Sometimes certain groups of children are not allowed to go to school. Malala Yousafzai is a Pakistani education activist. The Taliban (an Islamist extremist group) took control of her town in 2008 and banned girls from attending school. However, Yousafzai continued to go. She spoke out on behalf of education for girls and was shot by the Taliban in 2012. Yousafzai survived and remains a dedicated activist to this day.

Boys and girls study side by side at this school.

RAZUM/SHUTTERSTOCK.COM

In 2021 the Taliban took over the country of Afghanistan and banned girls from attending school past sixth grade. Activist groups are working hard to try to provide girls in Afghanistan alternative forms of education and reopen schools for girls.

Sometimes something as commonplace as having their period can keep students from attending school. In many places in the world, students lack sanitary and safe access to bathrooms and/or menstrual products, so they can't attend school when they are menstruating. There may also be a sense of shame, or cultural beliefs about periods being unclean, that lead students to stay home while menstruating.

Activists are working to provide students with menstrual products and education about the products to help them stay in school. Cloth pads, for example, can be washed and reused.
(MAIN) LOURDES BALDUQUE/GETTY IMAGES; (INSET) JENARI/SHUTTERSTOCK.COM

Adults Go to School Too

Children aren't the only ones who attend school. Although we might think of university, college or other post-secondary options as the only education choices for adults, that's not the case. People aged 18 or older who didn't graduate from secondary school have the option to do so, or to upgrade their skills, at community-based adult learning centers. Some courses are specifically for adults who are newcomers in the community and wish to learn the local language. Education for adults often offers flexible schedules or evening classes, allowing students to work or to care for children while attending school.

In the village of Phangane in India, there is a school just for grandmothers. As children, they weren't given the chance to attend school, but now they are. The grandmothers are happy and proud to attend school, just like their grandchildren.

INDRANIL MUKHERJEE/GETTY IMAGES

First Nations Schools

First Nations schools are schools that, although government-funded, are governed by the local First Nations themselves. In British Columbia, the First Nations Schools Association and the First Nations Education Steering Committee help support self-governed First Nations schools. Students at these schools receive an education that recognizes their unique culture and heritage in a nurturing environment. First Nations schools also play an important role in Indigenous language revitalization.

A curriculum developed by the First Nations Education Steering Committee and the BC Ministry of Education is now used throughout BC schools to teach students about Indigenous Peoples. Teachers who worked on that curriculum also created the First Peoples Principles of Learning. Defined by Indigenous Elders, scholars and knowledge keepers, these are general principles, not specific to any one Indigenous Nation, that distinguish teaching and learning approaches within Indigenous Nations.

This student is writing in Cree, which is one of the most widely spoken Indigenous languages in Canada.
HEMIS/ALAMY STOCK PHOTO

A Future of Inclusivity in Schools

Although schools have become more inclusive in recent years, there is still much work to do to ensure that all schools welcome everyone equally. One way many schools are moving toward even greater inclusivity is by creating gender-neutral restrooms. Rather than dividing students into two genders, gender-neutral restrooms (also known as universal or gender-inclusive restrooms) are meant for people of all genders while maintaining privacy.

1820s–1900s
Etiquette lessons
2000s–PRESENT
STEM gets added
to curriculum
2016–
PRESENT
SOGI in schools

1900s
Gendered home economics

Two

CURRICULUM

WHAT DO WE LEARN?

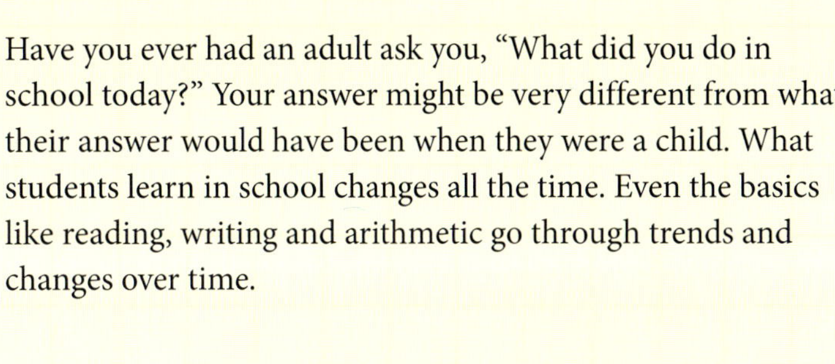

Have you ever had an adult ask you, "What did you do in school today?" Your answer might be very different from what their answer would have been when they were a child. What students learn in school changes all the time. Even the basics like reading, writing and arithmetic go through trends and changes over time.

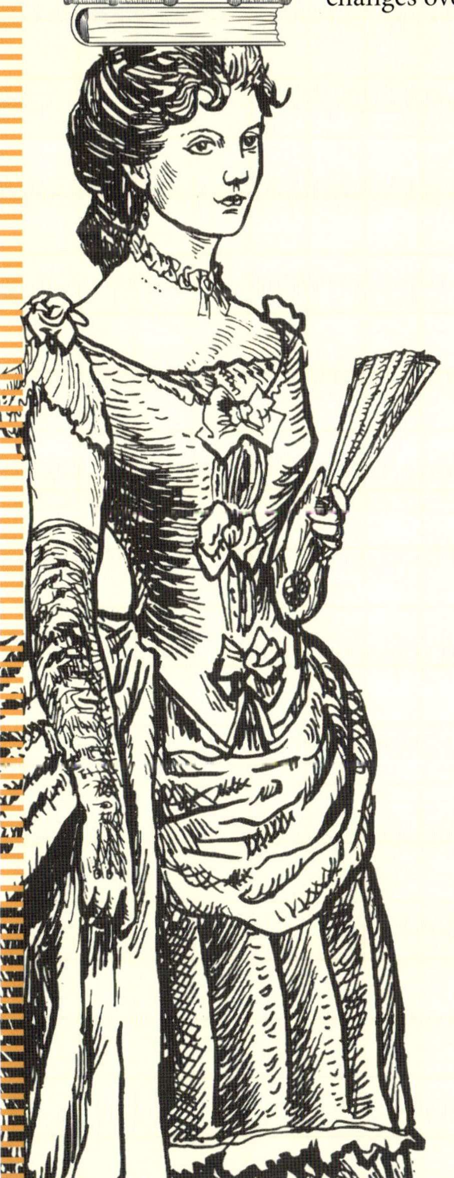

Learning from a Governess

Throughout history, many well-to-do families hired private teachers, called tutors. In Victorian England, governesses were a type of tutor who helped to raise *and* teach children (typically daughters) in wealthy families. Although governesses taught young boys, older boys were typically sent away to school.

Younger children were taught to read, write and do arithmetic, while older girls might be taught French, history, geography, art, piano and dance. Teaching ***etiquette*** and morals (such as saying prayers) was also considered the responsibility of a governess. And, of course, an important task was teaching daughters how to attract potential husbands! While this may seem odd to us now, women at the time did not have as many opportunities or rights as they do today, so a good marriage was serious business—and quite competitive.

ALEX74/SHUTTERSTOCK.COM

Attending an Elizabethan School

As we learned earlier, girls were most often educated at home, and their education was geared toward ***domesticity***, while boys were more likely to attend a formal school. We can look at Elizabethan England (1558–1603) as an example. Boys from wealthy families often attended private schools called grammar schools.

In Elizabethan grammar schools, children learned Latin. They also learned Greek and Roman literature. Younger boys were sometimes taught by older boys in addition to teachers. As a welcome break, the students were given time to play sports and take part in other nonacademic activities, like chess, running, wrestling, archery or drama.

Fun and games are key parts of school, after all. Schoolkids have played sports in many different eras and places throughout history. For example, the sport of modern rugby was famously invented by boys who attended Rugby School in England in 1823. It remains a popular sport to this day.

Home Economics and a Gendered Education

Curriculum for girls and boys continued to differ for a long time. The history of home economics tells a fascinating story of changing gender roles.

Home economics was developed in the United States in the early 1900s. It was designed to help improve conditions for women in the home by making domestic work easier, faster and safer. It was also meant to transform what was seen as "women's work" into a topic worthy of study and respect. Since home economics included topics of nutrition, food-service management, sanitation and product development, it also helped women attend universities and enter the workforce.

Home economics taught young women skills like cooking, sewing, childcare and creating a household budget.
JUPITERIMAGES/GETTY IMAGES

Apples and Teachers?

We don't know for sure how apples first became associated with school. However, historians believe that early American students in frontier towns sometimes gave apples to their teachers. Teachers didn't earn much money, and apples were a helpful (and delicious!) gift. The famous singer Bing Crosby's recording in 1939 of the song "An Apple for the Teacher" popularized the idea, and it has stuck to this day!

These days courses like textiles (sewing) and culinary arts (cooking) are typically included in conjunction with other life skills or applied technologies, such as woodworking or robotics. The subjects are not gendered, so all students have a chance to study these important subjects.
ROBERT KENT/GETTY IMAGES

Who Decides What We Learn?

Today the public school curriculum tends to be determined by governing bodies such as ministries of education. They may seek advice from other groups, such as teachers, education experts, multicultural groups and Indigenous communities. Then individual school boards, schools and teachers are responsible for applying and carrying out the curriculum. Therefore, the curriculum is different everywhere (even within the same country).

What's your favorite way to get active? Physical education (PE) or gym classes typically include sports like basketball. But some schools get creative, with options like yoga or cycling.
DRAZEN ZIGIC/GETTY IMAGES

Students can learn at home if they have an illness or injury that prevents them from going to school.
ROBERTO WESTBROOK/GETTY IMAGES

Classroom Alternatives

Traditional classrooms aren't always the best choice for every child or every family. In homeschooling, children learn from a parent or guardian. Tennis legends Venus and Serena Williams, for example, were both homeschooled by their father so they could dedicate more time to their tennis training.

There are many reasons why a family might choose homeschooling, including disabilities or special care needs, cultural concerns or even difficulty accessing a school. Children who are homeschooled might also participate in group activities with other homeschooled children.

Homeschooling isn't the only classroom alternative. Many children take classes online. Online learning means that students can be taught by certified teachers in a virtual setting. This lets students have flexibility in their learning while maintaining eligibility for graduation certificates.

An Education as Unique as You Are

Typically, public schools require students to take several core subjects like math, science and social studies. As students get older, they may have more choices in their education—allowing them to choose certain "electives," like computer programming or creative writing. Schools may also offer courses at different levels, like advanced-placement classes. Many school boards try to have options such as these for students with different interests and abilities.

As we have seen, the school experience is about more than just classes. Many schools offer enriching extracurricular activities such as sports teams and clubs. Getting involved in activities can mean making memories, acquiring experience for your résumé and, of course, having fun with friends!

Sometimes childhood friendships go down in history. Famous besties Bill Gates and Paul Allen met at school in 1968, where they bonded over a shared fascination with computers. They founded Microsoft together in 1975 and changed the world.

FG TRADE/GETTY IMAGES

Disabilities and Inclusivity in Schools

In the past, children with physical and/or intellectual disabilities were typically excluded from conventional schools. In Canada in the 1800s, for example, young people with special needs were often isolated or sent to live in institutions. By the 1920s institutions had become less common, and many schools created special-education classes for children with disabilities. Although they attended the same school, students in special-education classes were still segregated. In the 1970s and '80s, schools began to integrate classes.

Things have continued to improve, and inclusion is now the norm in Canada. However, schools still have a long way to go before they fully meet the physical, developmental, emotional and learning needs of every child. Disability advocates want to see more training for teachers, more funding and more resources for schools, which will help support everyone. Many students with disabilities continue to face discrimination. We can all help by learning more about these issues and unlearning stereotypes and misconceptions.

SOGI in Schools

Different people have different ideas of what should be included in school curriculums—and what *shouldn't* be included. One recent discussion has surrounded sexual orientation and gender identity (SOGI). As the British Columbia government explains, SOGI inclusivity in schools means welcoming everyone, valuing diversity and respecting differences when it comes to sexual orientation and gender identity.

SOGI isn't a curriculum but rather a resource and set of guidelines. The guidelines are meant to help stop bullying and harassment and make the school environment a safe place for ***2SLGBTQ+*** students as well as ***heterosexual*** and ***cisgender*** students. There are many ways SOGI practices can be used in schools, such as allowing students to self-identify (including their names and chosen ***pronouns***) and dress in a way that corresponds with their gender identity.

SOGI principles and practices have been used in BC schools since 2016 but have recently been getting a lot of attention. Not everyone supports them. There are many myths and misunderstandings about SOGI, and it has many vocal opponents. In 2023, for example, thousands of people protested against SOGI principles and practices in BC schools. However, thousands more showed up in support of SOGI.

You may be surprised to learn which books have been banned or challenged throughout history. Many classic and famous books fall into this category.
RICHARD BAILEY/GETTY IMAGES

Hidden Schools, Secret Students

Sometimes people have taken extraordinary measures to help make education possible. For example, before slavery was abolished in the United States, enslaved Black children sometimes learned to read and write in secret schools. Literacy (knowing how to read and write) gives people power, and enslavers did not want Black people to have power. During World War II, many Jews in Eastern Europe were forced to live in ghettos and later in prisons known as concentration camps, and children were not allowed to attend school. But secret schools existed in the ghettos—sometimes disguised as soup kitchens—for Jewish children to continue their education.

Banned Books in Schools

Another current curriculum controversy surrounds the topic of books. Once again, different groups of people have different ideas of what sorts of books are and are not appropriate for students. This includes both books in school libraries and those read as part of the curriculum. In recent years there has been an increase in calls to ban certain books in schools in the United States and Canada. Commonly challenged themes include sexuality, 2SLGBTQ+ topics and gender diversity.

For example, in 2022 a group of parents in Beaufort, South Carolina, in the United States tried to ban 97 books from school libraries. But instead of banning the books, community volunteers, teachers and librarians decided to read and discuss the books, and then took part in a vote. They decided that the vast majority of the challenged books should remain on the shelves.

Many people are speaking out in favor of challenged books, believing it is important to read and write about the diversity in the world around us, and to discuss complicated and current topics. There are even celebrations commemorating banned and challenged books. Banned Books Week and Freedom to Read Week, for example, celebrate intellectual freedom and access to information.

How Do We Learn to Read?

Do you remember learning how to read, and how powerful it feels? The world opens up to us when we can understand the written words all around us!

Many children find learning to read challenging, and more than half of Americans aged 16 to 74 read below a sixth-grade level. The standard approach in American schools in recent decades has been to look for context cues (like what's happening in a book's pictures) rather than being explicitly taught how to decode text (meaning how to sound out each word) or use phonics (learning the sounds that letters and groups of letters make). However, according to scientific research, we need decoding and phonics when we're learning how to read. Many schools, districts and teachers are now having important discussions about how they should teach reading.

JESSICA MIELKE/GETTY IMAGES

A Changing Curriculum for a Changing World

Curriculums will always change to reflect a changing world and prepare young people for a changing job market. Subjects and courses continue to be developed, and what we see as controversial today may not be controversial tomorrow.

In the past few decades, for example, we have seen the rise of STEM (science, technology, engineering and math) in classrooms. STEM education in schools includes things like learning the scientific method or how to code. Experts believe we will likely also see more climate and environmental education in the curriculums of the future, as we continue to adapt to a warming world. Many school boards are committed to having classes that deal with these topics.

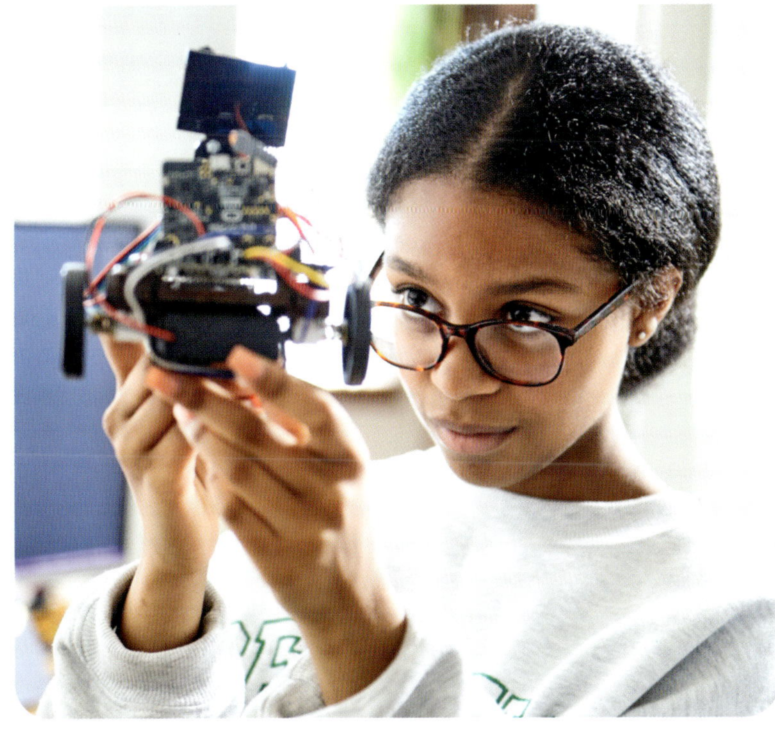

Do you love science? Some schools have science fairs where students present science projects they have created.
TARA MOORE/GETTY IMAGES

ELVA ETIENNE/GETTY IMAGES

And just as there are new additions to curriculums, there will also be things taken away. This, too, can be controversial. For example, several Canadian provinces have removed cursive writing from school curriculums, making it optional. However, the province of Ontario recently decided to bring cursive back to the mandatory school curriculum.

Why bring cursive back? Some education experts believe cursive writing is still a valuable skill that can help develop our brains and encourage learning, even in our current age of computer use. One scientific study found that writing in cursive may help us remember better than typing on a keyboard.

Cursive writing became less popular when typewriters were invented and less popular again with the rise of computers.
MILJKO/GETTY IMAGES

AI Comes to Class

Will artificial intelligence (AI) software change education? No one knows for sure. New guidelines, policies and penalties are being used by schools and teachers to discourage students from cheating by using AI chatbots for homework. They're also using tools and technology to catch AI-generated text in student assignments like essays. Other teachers are finding creative ways to use AI as a strategic tool with students as they navigate this new world together. Understanding and thinking critically about AI is part of today's—and tomorrow's—***digital literacy*** skill set.

3RD CENTURY BCE
First primary schools
in Ancient Rome
REFILL
2020
Learning from
home during
COVID pandemic
COMPOST

PAST, PRESENT AND FUTURE
Indigenous land-based learning

TODAY
Climate-focused schools

THREE

MORE THAN A BUILDING

WHERE DO WE LEARN?

Close your eyes and imagine your school. Is it old or new? Does it have a playground and ***portables***? Schools can be tiny one-room structures surrounded by countryside, or tall multistory buildings in the middle of bustling cities. Schools can be tree stumps in a circle in a forest clearing, or a collection of computers all connected remotely. There's no such thing as "normal"—schools are wherever students learn!

VADIM_NEFEDOV/GETTY IMAGES

Field trip! Learning out and about in nature, like these kids, can be educational—and super fun.
SOLSTOCK/GETTY IMAGES

Classrooms in Ancient Rome

School looked quite different in ancient times. Although ancient Rome had schools, there weren't designated school buildings. Poorer teachers often held classes outdoors, on street corners or in public squares or marketplaces. Wealthier teachers sometimes rented rooms to use as classrooms. These rooms might even have been at the back of a store. (As we learned in chapter 1, the wealthiest students were tutored at home.) Students often sat on stools, either in rows or in a semicircle around the teacher. There were no desks, so students held waxed writing tablets on their laps. Since educational equipment was expensive and relatively rare, there were few books or writing implements. Students wrote on their waxed tablets with something sharp, like a piece of metal, bone or wood. Occasionally students used reed pens.

Indigenous Land-Based Education

As we can see, there doesn't need to be a school building for learning to happen. For thousands of years, Indigenous Elders have taught their children through the practice of land-based education (or land-based learning).

This practice involves learning on the land as well as *from* the land—it is not simply learning done outdoors. Land-based learning is a multifaceted way of sharing knowledge, in which Elders and knowledge keepers lovingly and thoughtfully pass down their knowledge of the land, as well as their stories, languages, histories, cultures and traditions from generation to generation. Land-based learning is based on a deep sense of respect and connection with the land. Knowledge learned on the land, with the land, is specific to each area.

Despite colonization and residential schools (see chapter 1), land-based education continues today and will continue well into the future. This ongoing practice is a testament to the strength and resilience of Indigenous Peoples.

One of the aims of land-based education today is to honor and renew the relationship Indigenous Peoples have with the land, which was, and continues to be, damaged by colonizers and settlers. There are many different examples of land-based learning activities in which young people can participate. For example, they may learn how to cook traditional meals made from local ingredients, while learning the ingredients' importance to the land and their culture.

Camas bulbs were once an important traditional food for Coast Salish peoples. The bulbs are again being harvested and cooked.
(MAIN) KIMBERLY CAUVEL/NORTHWEST INDIAN FISHERIES COMMISSION; (INSET) SARYCHEVA OLESIA/SHUTTERSTOCK.COM

H. ARMSTRONG ROBERTS/GETTY IMAGES

Backpacks

One of the most iconic parts of any school outfit is the trusty backpack. But you might be surprised to learn that they're a very recent school staple! Backpacks as we know them today weren't popular in schools until the 1980s. Before that, students carried their books loose, or held together with a leather strap (like a belt). These days, backpacks have special pockets for technology and water bottles, and some even have wheels!

Early American Schools

The first public school in what would later become the United States opened in Boston, Massachusetts, in 1635. Boston Latin School was a boys-only secondary school originally made up of several buildings. The school's focus was to prepare young men for university.

In the late 1800s and early 1900s, there were numerous American schools. Many were one-room schoolhouses that could be described as utilitarian (which means they were designed to be useful but not attractive). These were not cheerful buildings. Desks were typically fixed to the floor in rows and could not be moved. Like most people's homes at this time, schools often didn't even have bathrooms! Students used outhouses instead.

However, around the turn of the century, experts started to put more emphasis on lighting, heating and ventilation, making schools brighter and more comfortable and with healthier airflow.

The postwar years between 1945 and 1960 brought a ***baby boom***, leading to more children in American schools than ever before. Mid-century schools didn't only try to meet students' physical needs but also their emotional needs. School buildings began to be designed as welcoming and friendly places. They might, for example, have interior courtyards, decorative design features and landscaping.

The next time you're in class, take a second to look around your classroom and see it with fresh eyes. What types of technology exist? Has your teacher added colorful art to the walls? Do you have modular furniture that gets moved around? How do you think your classroom would have looked 50 or even 100 years ago?
SEVENTYFOUR/GETTY IMAGES

Today's Classrooms

Classrooms today are a far cry from the dark, utilitarian buildings of the past. Although every school is different, classroom design of the 21st century embraces color, decoration, natural light and furniture designed for comfort and flexibility. Instead of furniture nailed to the floor, contemporary classroom furniture is often modular and adaptable, so teachers and students can use it in ways that work for them. Desks, tables and chairs can be moved around depending on the day's activities. Classrooms can have different areas (or "zones") for different learning purposes, like working independently or coming together on the carpet.

Today's classrooms feature much more technology too. Classroom technology includes computers, of course, but also technology we might not always think of, like updated ventilation systems to help reduce the spread of illnesses and improve air quality.

Although there have been advancements, far too many schools in Canada and the United States are in disrepair or overcrowded. Portables, for example, were originally intended to be a temporary solution of the 1970s, '80s and '90s. At many schools, they became permanent additions.

Approximately one-third of public schools in the United States have portables. Does yours?
JARVELL JARDEY/GETTY IMAGES

SIRIDHATA/GETTY IMAGES

NOSYSTEM IMAGES/GETTY IMAGES

School Design and Crime Prevention

A lot goes into the design of a building, including features to prevent crime and violence. For example, fences and gates can be used to stop people from entering certain areas and guide them to other areas. Good lighting may discourage crime by increasing visibility.

Sometimes school design is contested. For example, classrooms with glass walls are thought to increase engagement, transparency and natural lighting. But these walls also raise safety and privacy concerns. For instance, in the case of a lockdown drill or shooting, clear glass walls make it much harder for students and staff to hide. Frosted glass and window coverings can help alleviate some of these concerns.

It is an unfortunate reality that contemporary school design must consider the possibility of school shootings. But school design is far from being the only defensive strategy when it comes to these tragic incidents—gun-control policies and mental-health supports would be key preventive measures.

Unequal School Districts

Sadly, to this day children experience great inequities when it comes to the types of school they attend. You may be surprised to learn that *where* a student lives can determine the type of school they attend—even within the public school system.

In the United States, the way school districts are divided means that some districts are wealthier and others are poorer. Since ***property taxes*** help fund schools, wealth inequality in a given neighborhood leads to wealth inequality in that neighborhood's schools. Racial inequality is also at play here, as Black, Indigenous and students of color are more likely to live in poorer areas and attend poorer schools. This is a big deal, because school funding has huge consequences. Students who attend schools with more funding are more likely to graduate and even to earn more money as adults.

In Lower Merion Township, a suburban community in Pennsylvania, students are mostly white. The district spends $27,818 per student each year. In nearby Philadelphia, Pennsylvania, one of the poorest large cities in the United States, the students are mostly nonwhite: 47 percent are Black and 24 percent are Hispanic/Latino. The district spends $15,066 per student each year. This is just one example of inequality in school funding.

Shannen Koostachin's Fight for Safe and Comfy Schools

Inequality exists in Canadian schools too. Schools on First Nations reserves struggle with an ongoing lack of funding. In 2000, in Ontario, the Attawapiskat First Nation's elementary school was forced to close due to toxic contamination dating back to 1979. The community's 400 children had no school apart from temporary portable trailers without proper insulation and ventilation. Over years of use the trailers deteriorated and became infested with mice and black mold. Many students dropped out of school.

Shannen Koostachin was a student there who was determined that she and her classmates should have a new school. Along with other children and community members, she wrote to the federal government, spread the word on social media, met with government officials and delivered a speech at the University of Toronto. In 2008 she was nominated for the International Children's Peace Prize for her work campaigning for "safe and comfy schools." Tragically, Koostachin died in a car accident in 2010 at age 15. But her work continued and became the largest youth-led rights movement in Canada's history. Thanks to Koostachin's work, a new school was built in Attawapiskat in 2014.

During the COVID-19 pandemic, many students had to study at home and take their classes online.
PAUL BIRIS/GETTY IMAGES

Learning from Home

In March 2020 schools were shut down due to the COVID-19 pandemic. Teachers, parents and students had to adapt quickly to online learning. Not surprisingly, this was a big challenge. While virtual learning was important to help stop the spread of COVID-19, the sudden shift caused many problems. Experts believe that lockdown and distance learning harmed the most vulnerable students, who often didn't have the necessary technology at home for virtual learning. Distance learning also relied on parents helping their children learn, which wasn't possible for many families. As a result, inequities that already existed were made worse.

Virtual learning can be a great option for some students. Experts hope we can learn from the lessons the COVID-19 pandemic taught us so we can improve distance learning in the future.

Learning in Nature

Nature schools (also known as forest schools or outdoor schools) have gained popularity in North America in recent years, and there's a good chance their popularity will continue to grow. During the pandemic, many parents and teachers embraced outdoor learning, as viruses are less likely to spread outside. Classes in nature were one creative way to help slow the spread of COVID-19 while also giving young people a much-needed break from screens.

However, nature schools aren't a new idea. In Scandinavian countries like Denmark, forest schools have been around for many years. The nature-school approach is based on the belief that time outside in nature has huge value for our mental, emotional and physical health. Often learning is play-based and hands-on, with an emphasis on exploration and curiosity.

Climate-Focused Schools

Like nature schools, ***sustainable*** schools are not a new concept. In the 1990s progressive, eco-friendly schools focused on sustainable school design and building principles. Sustainability can mean many different things for schools, such as:

avoiding toxic materials in construction

using renewable energy

including water-bottle refill stations

using living walls and vertical greenhouses

constructing green roofs

composting food scraps (sometimes even with worm bins!)

tending to school gardens

using less water (maybe even collecting and reusing rainwater)

recycling, but also reducing the amount of waste created

Sustainable school design is still important and will continue to be in the future. Being climate-minded, however, can—and must—go even further. Just like other buildings, schools of the present and future need to be designed for a warming planet. Many old buildings, schools included, weren't built with extreme heat in mind and lack adequate cooling strategies. In British Columbia, heat waves in recent years saw some classrooms with temperatures ranging from 84 to 91°F (29 to 33°C). Extreme heat can impair learning and threaten our health. In many areas of Canada and the United States, school districts don't have adequate funds for air-conditioning and are struggling to figure out how to cool schools.

A warming planet also leads to increased wildfires, smoky skies and air-quality concerns. Schools need to grapple with these issues to ensure that the air in school buildings is clean and safe for students. Air purifiers and good ventilation systems can help.

Many schools around the world are taking steps to reduce the amount of waste they create and are opting to reuse and recycle whenever possible. Is your school one of them? Consider starting a club to help your school go low-waste and protect the planet! SKYNESHER/GETTY IMAGES

School playgrounds can be used and loved by all kids in the area!
HALYTSKYI OLEXANDR/SHUTTERSTOCK.COM

Accessible Schools

Today's and tomorrow's schools also need to improve their ***accessibility*** standards, so that all children are able to learn—and play. Accessible playgrounds come at a cost, but are one tangible way to support equity and inclusion, allowing children to exercise, socialize and enjoy time outdoors. Since many children enjoy playgrounds outside of school hours, accessible school playgrounds benefit the entire community.

A unique example of accessibility are communication boards, which feature facial expressions, gestures, symbols and words. Verbal communication can be challenging for some children (including many on the autism spectrum), and these boards allow children to communicate more easily. A child can point to the word and symbol for "sick," for example, to tell a peer or caregiver that they aren't feeling well. The Lester B. Pearson School Board in Quebec is installing communication stations in all of its school playgrounds.

Take a minute to examine this communication board. Could you use it to put together a thought or phrase?
VANPRASAD/SHUTTERSTOCK.COM

What Do You Wear to School?

School uniforms date back to the year 1222 in England—at least, that's the earliest recorded use of them that we know of. Today we tend to associate school uniforms with private schools. Some people like school uniforms because they think they help foster concentration and community, and prevent bullying based on clothing. Others dislike them, however, because they think uniforms reduce students' ability to express themselves.

Many schools have dress codes, and these too can be controversial. In recent years dress codes have been criticized for being outdated and sexist, unfairly targeting female students and also blaming them for distracting male students. Dress codes can be racist as well, such as targeting and policing Black students' hairstyles. Schools across Canada and the United States are rethinking and updating their dress codes to allow individual expression and take into consideration nonbinary and diverse students.

19TH CENTURY–TODAY
Summer vacation
19TH CENTURY
School bell
20TH CENTURY–TODAY
Homework debate

FOUR

SCHOOL TIME

WHEN DO WE LEARN?

Have you ever wondered why we go to school when we do? Why do most schools close for two months of summer vacation? Why does the school day start and stop at the time it does? Just like every other aspect of education, when we learn has a storied past that has changed over the years.

A Typical School Day

These days a typical school day in the United States and Canada spans roughly six hours. For kindergarten (the year before first grade), students might attend a full-day (six-hour) program or a partial-day program. These typical hours were developed years ago and haven't changed much. They were chosen so children still had time during the day to help out at home or on the family farm.

However, start and end times have shifted somewhat since then. A school day that starts after nine o'clock in the morning creates challenges for parents who work outside the house and have to get their children to school. That's why, in the 1970s, many schools shifted to earlier start times.

FATCAMERA/GETTY IMAGES

The Best Part of the School Day?

What's your favorite part of the school day? If you say recess, you're not alone! Recess isn't just fun—it's also healthy! A break from ***academics*** helps you mentally, physically, socially and emotionally. In the United States, elementary schoolkids are entitled to an average of 27 minutes of recess daily.

Saved by the Bell!

The start and end of the school day has been marked by a bell for hundreds of years. These days we are used to the electric sounds over a school's PA system that might be more reminiscent of a buzzer than the tolling of a bell. However, in the olden days (such as in 19th-century one-room schoolhouses), the school bell was quite literally a bell. The teacher would stand and ring a handbell to signal the start of school. Bells have a long and storied history in marking the passage of time, being used not only in schools but also in churches and factories.

NEW AFRICA/SHUTTERSTOCK.COM

In Finland recess is much longer than it is in the United States and Canada, and school puts more emphasis on playtime and less on academics until students are older.
FLY VIEW PRODUCTIONS

Lunchtime!

When school lasts for the better part of the day, lunchtime is a necessity! And like many other aspects of school, lunchtime has changed throughout the centuries. For example, pioneer children who attended school in the 1870s in Washington State brought lunch from home or walked home for lunch if they lived close enough to the school. Packed lunches might have included jam or meat sandwiches, bread with lard, or hard-boiled eggs.

In the United States in the 1920s, schools started to include lunchrooms, and there were some volunteer-run school lunch programs. During the Great Depression of the 1930s, children were going hungry, and the government stepped in with more school lunch programs. Throughout the years, school lunch foods have become more varied to reflect the country's diverse population. These days some students buy or receive a lunch at school, others bring packed lunches from home.

Some students, staff and parents believe that lunchtime isn't long enough to eat and enjoy a proper meal, especially now that more schools offer meals that students stand in line to get. In the United States, the recommended eating time is at least 30 minutes, but many students don't get that much time. In other countries, such as France, lunchtime is much longer, allowing for a more relaxed eating experience.
WESTEND61/GETTY IMAGES

Can you believe that even school lunches have been controversial? There have been many discussions and disagreements between groups over how school lunches should be funded, what they should cost, what sorts of foods the meals should include, what kind of nutritional standards lunches should meet and whether fast-food companies and other corporations should be involved in school lunches. In 1981 the United States government, in order to save money, proposed changing school-lunch nutritional guidelines so that ketchup could be considered a vegetable. After lots of criticism, this idea was scrapped.

In 2020 school lunches made the news again. When schools closed during the COVID-19 pandemic, many children missed out on physical activity, health services, mental health supports, and free or low-cost lunches they wouldn't be able to get otherwise. For some children, school lunch is the only nourishing meal of the day they can count on. In some places, school meals were delivered to students. According to UNICEF, 370 million children around the world were at risk of missing school meals due to the pandemic.

After-school time means fun and enrichment. You might hang out with friends and get involved in extracurricular activities like clubs, arts and sports. You might also take part in tutoring (either being tutored by or tutoring other kids), volunteering or working at a part-time job.
FANGXIANUO/GETTY IMAGES

What Are You Doing After School?

Earlier in this chapter, we learned that school start times shifted to take into account working parents. But what about school end times? The typical school day ends a full two hours before the typical workday does, so the timing gets tricky when parents work outside the house.

The term ***latchkey kid*** is believed to date back to the 1940s. It referred to kids left home alone when their fathers were serving in the Second World War and their mothers had to work outside the home. However, the term became popular in the 1970s and '80s, when more parents began working outside the house on a long-term basis. Single-parent households also became more common. Since these children and teens (who belonged to Generation X) were alone for so long, they became known for being independent and resilient. However, some felt neglected and lonely.

These days, daycares and before- and after-school programs are common, meaning fewer kids go unsupervised. Sometimes these programs are expensive and have limited spaces available, but new government initiatives are trying to make them more accessible.

Cyberbullying

Gone are the days when bullying existed only in the schoolyard. Technology, such as cell phones and social media, makes it all too easy for bullying to continue beyond school hours. Experts call this type of bullying cyberbullying, and an estimated 30 percent of Canadian youth report having been victims. Cyberbullying can have serious legal consequences. Making threats, sharing intimate images, identity theft and intimidation are all examples of criminal charges associated with cyberbullying, according to Canada's *Criminal Code*. Schools are trying to prevent cyberbullying before it even starts by introducing programs to teach young people digital literacy and wellness.

Learning on Your Own Time

Some unique schools allow students more flexibility in the timing of their learning. In the SPARTS program at Magee Secondary School in Vancouver, British Columbia, students study part-time while also participating at an elite level in sports or arts. The word SPARTS is a creative mash-up of the words "sports" and "arts." The program allows students to pursue excellence in their chosen fields without missing out on academics. Students have to apply for the program and must demonstrate a high level of dedication and discipline.

At Thomas Haney Secondary School in Maple Ridge, British Columbia, learning is self-directed. Schedules are flexible and tailored to the student, allowing students with different learning methods to thrive.

It can be hard to balance your passions with your schoolwork. Thankfully, some schools make it easier to do that.
MARK EDWARD ATKINSON/
GETTY IMAGES

Time for Homework

It probably won't surprise you to learn that many kids hate homework. But would it surprise you to learn that throughout history, many adults hated homework too? The battle over homework has been raging for years.

In the early 1900s several education theorists argued that homework could harm children's physical and mental health. In the 1930s some people even considered homework to be child labor! However, some educational theorists believed that certain types of homework (like reading or self-directed projects) could be beneficial. Homework surged in popularity in the 1950s and then again in the 1980s in the United States. The debate continues today.

The subject of homework is controversial, with some parents and teachers in favor of the practice, and others firmly against it. Still others believe in a happy medium, advocating for homework that is meaningful for reinforcing concepts and teaching students to think critically. What do you believe?
JAVIER ZAYAZ/GETTY IMAGES

How Do Kids Get to School?

How do you get to school? Maybe you walk or ride your bike. Maybe you get a lift from your mom or dad, or take the bus. In Canada about three-quarters of kids rely on a motorized vehicle of some sort to get to school, while 22 percent walk and 4 percent ride a bike.

Kids around the world get to school in countless different ways, including by boat, subway, snowmobile or gondola. Some ways are treacherous, such as hiking along steep mountainsides or crossing unsafe makeshift bridges. Trips to school are long and tiring for those who live in rural areas. No matter where they live, all kids deserve to travel to school safely.

As tempting as it might be to keep them close, our phones don't belong in our beds. Recent research in Norway suggests that screen time in bed can affect students' sleep.
ANASTASIA BABENKO/GETTY IMAGES

Changing Thoughts About the School Day

Just as school start and end times have shifted over the decades, they may shift again in the future. Teenagers aren't night owls by coincidence: a real biological change happens in adolescence that makes teens tend to stay up later at night and wake up later in the morning. This means most schools' current start times are too early for many teens to learn optimally. Many people believe school should start later, allowing teens a greater chance to thrive.

In the fall of 2016, high schools in Seattle decided to start classes about one hour later—at 8:45 a.m. rather than 7:50 a.m. This change meant reorganizing bus schedules and extracurricular activities. But the change was welcomed by teens, who were able to sleep longer in the mornings. Research shows extra sleep may improve attendance and help teenagers achieve better grades.

Specialized Boarding Schools

For some students, school doesn't end when the day's lessons end. Boarding schools have been around in different forms for hundreds of years, and they still exist today.

Highly specialized schools sometimes offer day or boarding options because children travel from far away to attend the school. For example, Perkins School for the Blind in Watertown, Massachusetts, teaches students aged 3 to 22 and offers living facilities for those aged 12 and older. Along with specialized education, students have the opportunity to participate in various extracurricular activities like sports and clubs.

PER-ANDERS PETTERSSON/GETTY IMAGES

No More Snow Days?

If you live in an area that gets snow, you might have experienced the excitement of a snow day—that's when school is closed due to heavy snowfall. With online learning now a reality, snow days may be replaced with virtual learning days. In some school districts, this is already happening. However, many people are fighting this idea, arguing that snow days are a fun rite of passage for kids.

Snow is not the only ***extreme weather event*** that forces school closures. In our warming world, extreme heat and smoky air from wildfires are two key concerns that can cause in-person schools to close.

Have you ever heard the saying "There's no such thing as bad weather, just bad clothing"? This expression is popular in Nordic countries, which are often snowy and cold. With the right gear, snowy days (and rainy days!) can be fun and comfortable.

ARIEL SKELLEY/GETTY IMAGES

Is the last day of school the most exciting day of the school year? A lot of students would say yes!
MONKEYBUSINESSIMAGES/GETTY IMAGES

School's Out for the Summer!

Have you ever wondered why we go back to school in the fall and have vacation in the summer? It wasn't always this way. Many schools used to operate year-round, with occasional breaks.

Although we might assume that in the olden days, children were needed at home to work on farms during the summer, this is only partially true. It's true that children were needed at home, and their school attendance tended to vary with the changing seasons. But the busiest seasons on farms are springtime (when crops are planted) and fall (when crops are harvested). So why did summer become the season for school vacations?

American historians tell us that in the days before air-conditioning, schools were often too hot in summer for students and staff to be comfortable. Plus, wealthy urban families tended to go on long trips during the summer months. In the late 19th century, these factors (as well as the desire to give teachers and students a longer break) gave rise to the summer vacation. This decision also helped standardize the school year, meaning that schools in different areas had similar vacation times.

But not every school has a long summer vacation. Some modern schools run year-long, with different, shorter holidays throughout the year rather than one long holiday.

The Summer Slide

Not everyone thinks that the summer vacation is a smart idea. Some education experts believe the long summer break is harmful to students, as it interrupts their routine and makes it easy to forget what they learned in the school year. The theory that many students lose the academic gains they make during the school year after a vacation is sometimes called "the summer slide." This summer slide disproportionately affects students from low-income families who may not have access to activities like academic summer camps.

But other education experts believe that worries about the summer slide are exaggerated. They believe that such study results fail to provide a clear picture and that companies may even use the concept of the summer slide to sell services and programs like tutoring or activity books. It's also important to remember that learning isn't only about academics. Traveling, spending time with family and good old-fashioned play are all excellent ways to continue our education in other areas.

?
5TH CENTURY BCE
Socratic method

Today is...
19TH-
20TH CENTURY
Corporal
punishment

TODAY
Decolonizing
education

FIVE

TEACHING METHODS

HOW DO WE LEARN?

Do you have to memorize the times tables? You know, $1 \times 2 = 2$, $2 \times 2 = 4$, $3 \times 2 = 6$ and so on. Do you sound out new words when you're reading or use the illustrations to help? It's important to ask why we learn the way do. How do teachers teach? And how could we improve the way information is taught so it benefits everyone?

FUTURE
New learning methods

Questions and Answers

Teaching methods have evolved over time. The ancient Greek philosopher Socrates developed a unique way of teaching so famous that it is still well known today. It's called the Socratic method, and it relies on conversation between the teacher and the student, the teacher asking the student many questions. This questioning encourages the student to think deeply and critically about a topic rather than simply memorizing information without truly understanding it.

That's not to say that memorization itself is bad. Memorizing information by practicing or repeating it can help our brains learn and retain information. Just like the Socratic method, memorization can be useful and has its place in learning.

WIKIMEDIA COMMONS/PUBLIC DOMAIN

Students in ancient Rome wrote on wax tablets like this.
GIAMKA/SHUTTERSTOCK.COM

How Kids Learned in Ancient Roman Schools

In ancient Rome students of different ages and abilities attended school at the same time, so they had different lessons to work on individually. Students memorized and recited poetry and other texts, and practiced writing by copying out sentences. Memorizing information by repeating it (like copying out sentences) is sometimes called rote learning. Older students were trained in public speaking and rhetoric (the art of persuasion and debate). School in ancient Rome was strict, and students were often punished physically.

How Kids Learned in Early American Schools

Historical records show us that American pioneer children in the 19th century studied from readers, which were like textbooks. Readers contained the alphabet, as well as poems, stories and nonfiction lessons in subjects such as history and ***philosophy***. Like children in ancient Rome, American students memorized and recited passages.

And like teachers in ancient Rome, 19th-century American teachers were strict! Students who misbehaved, didn't complete their work or even just failed to answer a question correctly could be punished by having no recess or by staying after school. They might also have to clean the blackboard, sit in a corner or write lines (writing the same thing over and over). And teachers could physically punish students, such as by hitting them with a ruler.

Some North American schools at this time also had some practices that might strike us nowadays as odd. For example, students' hands and fingernails were inspected daily for dirt. Even their teeth could be inspected and had to be clean!

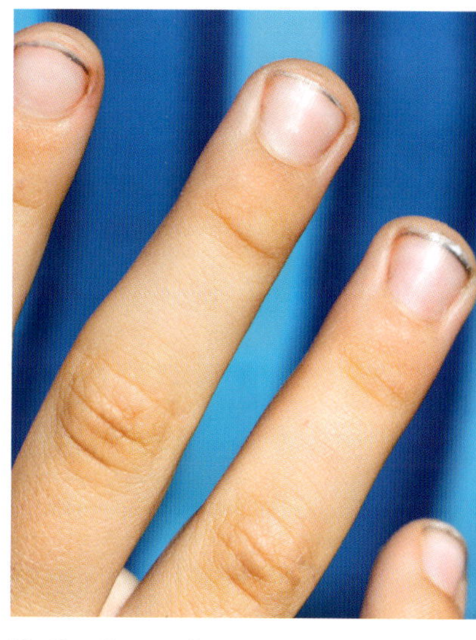

No dirty fingernails allowed at school!
ELENA TITOVA/GETTY IMAGES

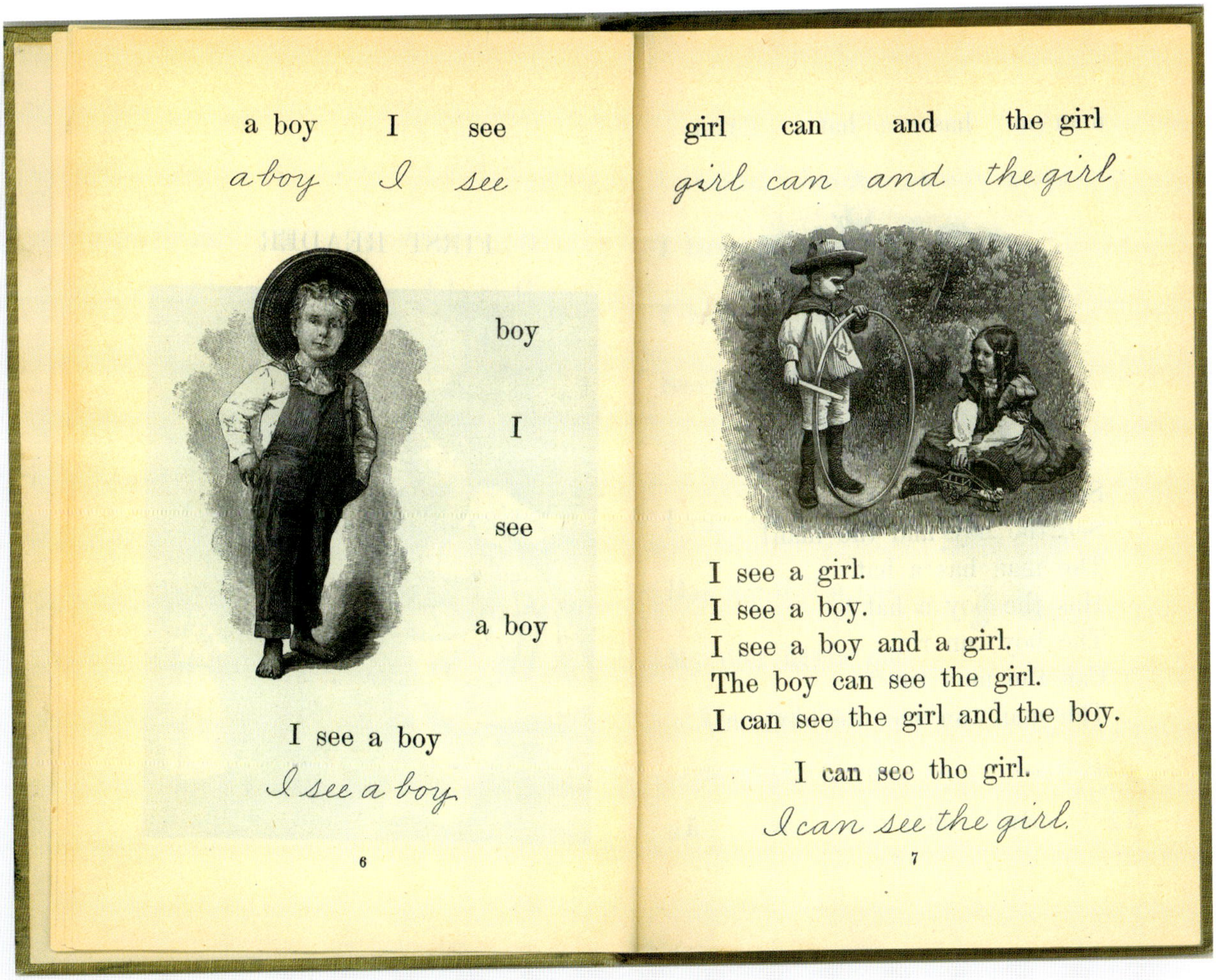

a boy I see
a boy I see

boy
I
see
a boy

I see a boy
I see a boy

6

girl can and the girl
girl can and the girl

I see a girl.
I see a boy.
I see a boy and a girl.
The boy can see the girl.
I can see the girl and the boy.

I can sec tho girl.
I can see the girl.

7

Books known as *readers*, like this one, were a bit like textbooks. They were popular in 19th-century schools in the United States. This one has repetitive passages to help build confidence in young students.
UNIVERSITY OF WASHINGTON/WIKIMEDIA COMMONS/PUBLIC DOMAIN

Schools can offer specialized curriculums. In Canada, French immersion programs offer curriculum instruction in French rather than English, allowing students to become bilingual.
SKYNESHER/GETTY IMAGES

Changing Views of Teaching and Learning

There have been many different ***educational theories*** over the years. Three examples are behavioral learning theory, experiential learning theory and connectivism learning theory.

Behavioral learning theory came about in the 19th century. According to this theory, students learn by interacting with their environments, and strategies like positive reinforcement (rewarding students for correct answers) are used to help students learn. For example, a teacher might give out a sticker or a certificate for a job well done.

Experiential learning theory came about in the 1980s. Its emphasis is on learning by "doing" and through hands-on experiences. Going on field trips and completing science lab experiments are two examples.

Connectivism learning theory came about in the early 2000s. According to this theory, students learn by forming connections. Technology, as well as strategies like collaboration and discussion, are used to help students learn. An example is a group project.

Are you wondering which educational theory your school or teacher uses? They might apply a combination of several different types of theories and strategies.

Student Activists

Students have power. Throughout time and around the world, student activists have made a difference in the world.

One example is Greta Thunberg. In 2018, at age 15, Thunberg started her School Strike for Climate outside the parliament in Sweden. The young environmentalist wanted leaders and policymakers to take action to mitigate climate change. She was soon joined by more activists, and her school strike became famous. Thunberg eventually returned to school but continued to strike every Friday, creating the Fridays for Future movement. She has met with many world leaders, spoken at international climate events and been nominated for the Nobel Peace Prize multiple times. Her work encouraged climate strikes in more than 160 countries around the world in September 2019. Thunberg has been diagnosed with a form of autism. She explains that being different in this way is a gift and a superpower, allowing her to focus her attention on her activism.

Another example is Ose Arheghan, who uses they/them pronouns and comes from Ohio. During high school and university, Arheghan fought for LGBTQ+ rights. Today they are an award-winning journalist and activist who focuses on queer and trans young people of color. In 2023 Arheghan was named the 12th Youth Observer to the United Nations.

Other famous examples of student activism in the United States included civil rights protests and anti–Vietnam War protests at universities during the 1960s. More recently, Black Lives Matter protests in the 2010s and 2020s have shone the spotlight on police violence against Black people.

EDWIN TAN/GETTY IMAGES

Developed by Dr. Maria Montessori in Italy in the 1890s and early 1900s, Montessori education is student-led. Children pursue their interests and curiosities at their own pace and in a hands-on way. Many Montessori preschools exist, and sometimes children have the option of a Montessori education in older years as well.
WIKIMEDIA COMMONS/PUBLIC DOMAIN

How Do You Learn?

Many public schools have moved toward methods that take into consideration students' different learning styles and development.

We all learn in different ways. Maybe you learn best when you can see information visually. Perhaps it's by listening to information. Maybe you find it easiest to take in new ideas by writing them down, taking notes or even doodling. Or maybe you enjoy learning by doing, keeping your body active. You might prefer one technique over another or a combination of techniques. Certain learning styles work well with some teaching styles and not with others. For example, if you learn best while moving, a teaching style that insists you sit still isn't a good match.

As you read through this list of trendy teaching tactics, ask yourself which best suit your unique personality and learning style. Perhaps you can use this knowledge to have a conversation with your parents and teachers about how you learn best.

Fidget items like these are often used by children with autism. They can help some students self-regulate and remain calm and comfortable in a classroom setting. Many schools and libraries offer sensory kits that contain items like fidget toys to help support people with diverse needs.
ANDRESWD/GETTY IMAGES

Collaboration and dialogue-based learning includes group projects and presentations.

Movement (such as stretching) can be used between lessons or built into the lessons themselves. Even furniture can be designed with movement in mind, allowing students to rock or wobble.

Hands-on and **experiential learning** could mean anything from a field trip to a demonstration by a guest speaker to a self-directed science project.

Tools that take into account students' unique **sensory needs** allows children to thrive in an environment that is comfortable for them. Examples include using noise-blocking headphones or fidget toys.

Incorporating **technology** means learning *how* to use technology, as well as learning critical thinking skills *while* using it. This includes digital literacy.

Social and emotional learning is thought to create a culture of kindness, promote collaboration, reduce emotional distress, teach healthy relationship skills and improve behavior. Examples of social and emotional learning in the classroom include teaching mindfulness and discussing emotions.

Gamification means incorporating elements of games and play (like points systems and badges) into learning opportunities. This tactic is thought to increase motivation and make learning more fun and engaging.

When it comes to standardized tests, students from poorer families do not always have the same resources for extra test prep that students from wealthier homes have. Alternative ways to assess a student's learning are reflections and reports, hands-on projects and frequent low-stakes quizzes.
KLAUS VEDFELT/GETTY IMAGES

What About Grades?

How do teachers know if students have learned the material they have been taught? How can we track students' progress? Do tests and letter grades benefit students and support learning? These are big questions—and experts don't always agree on the answers.

In early American schools, teachers commonly gave oral reports to parents about their children's progress. Then, in the early 1900s, American students (mostly in urban areas) began receiving report cards. In later years North American students received letter grades and/or a percentage (a number between 0 and 100). Another method, commonly associated with postsecondary education, is the 4.0 scale.

One controversial practice is scoring students on a bell curve. A certain number of each letter grade is given out by the teacher. A few students will receive the highest marks, a few students will receive the lowest marks, and most will be in the middle (creating a bell curve shape on a graph). Since this approach means your grade ultimately depends on how your classmates do, many people consider it unfair.

But what about grades in general? Are they helpful or harmful? Some education experts argue that grades encourage competition, comparison and even cheating. They say that by focusing too much on grades, we may forget to celebrate the spirit of learning. These experts believe schools should encourage curiosity and personal growth.

Several schools are changing their approaches to grading. In British Columbia, schools have recently shifted away from letter grades for students in kindergarten to ninth grade. Students are now evaluated on a proficiency scale, with four categories: emerging, developing, proficient and extending. ***Emerging*** signals that a student has an initial understanding of the concepts, while ***extending*** signals that a student has a sophisticated understanding. Learning is seen as a process, with no such thing as perfection. There is also a IE designation for insufficient evidence of learning (due to missed assignments, for example).

DUSAN STANKOVIC/GETTY IMAGES

Mistakes Versus Cheating

The *Magic School Bus*'s famous teacher, Ms. Frizzle, had it right when she advised us to take chances, make mistakes and get messy! Making mistakes is a normal part of the learning process and can actually be helpful. Research has shown that making and then fixing mistakes can help us learn more effectively. Mistakes do not mean failure! Try to remember that the next time you're worrying about a school assignment.

On the other hand, cheating *is* thought to interfere with the learning process. When a student cheats, the teacher can't accurately assess how much the student has learned or how the student can improve. Of course, students who cheat can also face serious academic consequences for this dishonest and unethical practice.

Decolonizing Education

Decolonization means working to undo colonizing practices. This process can happen in schools as educators question, challenge and change educational practices. Your school may be already doing some of these things. A few examples include:

- incorporating land acknowledgments, which recognize the Indigenous Peoples who were here before white settlers;
- incorporating local Indigenous languages in school signs and names;
- including (and displaying) Indigenous books, artwork, resources and other materials in school library collections;
- involving local Elders and Indigenous community members in classroom experiences and the school curriculum.

These are just a few of the many ways in which the school system can and needs to be decolonized. The education system as a whole was created by and for white settlers, so this is a huge undertaking. Decolonization in education also means changing the *way* we learn, not just changing *what* we learn about. Incorporating Indigenous ways of knowing means focusing on a child's whole being, so that we can show kindness and respect to everyone and collaborate with others. Even the way students are evaluated could be shifted away from the focus on competition. This process will take time and learning, not only for students but for educators. It will require education systems and governments to be open to the changes required for decolonization to happen.

These days many schools have Indigenous support workers who help provide cultural support to Indigenous students, as well as academic and social support.
RICHLEGG/GETTY IMAGES

What would you prefer to do, a hands-on robotics project or a book report? There is no right answer! Every person is different and has unique skills.
MONKEYBUSINESSIMAGES/GETTY IMAGES

The Future of How We Learn

How will students of the future learn? Here are a few predictions based on current trends.

Through student-centered learning, education may become more personalized, with a tailored approach to learning based on an individual student's unique needs and learning style. This may also mean that the curriculum is flexible and adaptive, with students helping to make decisions. For example, a student may get to choose which hands-on activity they complete during a lesson.

We will likely see more use of technology in the classroom, with students learning *about* technology as well as *through* technology. This also means we will need to address the ***digital divide***, in which some schools and students have more access to technology than others.

The way students learn may also be influenced by global awareness and understanding. Students learn how to become ***global citizens*** by learning about the world as a whole as well as how to become involved in their communities. We can learn beyond the classroom in creative and hands-on ways. This might include a nature-restoration project (see "Greening Schoolyards").

Greening Schoolyards

Many schools across the United States and Canada are transforming their schoolyards from drab asphalt to lush green oases. In New York City, a nonprofit organization has transformed more than 200 schoolyards into beautiful (and fun!) areas where students are happy to spend time. On Quadra Island in British Columbia, students and staff worked to restore a natural wetland at their school. And a school in Toronto recently undertook a ravine-restoration project, uncovering a natural stream that had been buried.

These projects don't just benefit students—they also help the environment. Green spaces mean more habitat for nearby wildlife and cooler temperatures in heat waves. Restoring streams and wetlands also helps reduce the risk of flooding. It's a great example of taking education outside the classroom to improve our communities.

Throughout this book, we have seen that school isn't only about tests or grades. School is about community, collaboration and creating a better world—together.

SDI PRODUCTIONS/GETTY IMAGES

What do you think schools of the future will be like? What do you think the students of tomorrow will think about the schools of today?
MILJKO/GETTY IMAGES

GLOSSARY

2SLGBTQ+—an acronym that stands for Two-Spirit, lesbian, gay, bisexual, transgender, queer or questioning, as well as any additional sexual orientations or gender identities not mentioned in the acronym

academic—relating to school or formal education (such as courses that people study)

accessibility—refers to the design of products, services or environments so they can be easily used or accessed by people with disabilities

activist—a person who takes action to create change by doing such things as writing letters or protesting

artificial intelligence (AI)—computer systems that can do tasks that once required human intelligence, such as solving problems and making decisions

assimilating—to absorb into the cultural tradition of a population or group

baby boom—the increase in the birth rate in Canada and the United States following World War II, leading to a higher population (people born during this time belong to the "baby boomer" generation)

cisgender—a term (sometimes shortened to cis) that describes a person whose gender identity matches the sex that they were assigned at birth (in contrast, when someone's gender identity does not match up with the sex they were assigned at birth, they are described as transgender)

colonization—the process of one group of people taking control of the land, resources and culture of the people who first lived there

cultural genocide—the process of intentionally destroying a culture (even without physical violence), such as by banning or destroying language, artifacts, traditions and activities

curriculum—the set of courses, created from ideas, societal norms and goals, that students are taught

decolonization—the process of working to undo and remove colonizing practices and systems and instead honor, incorporate and assert Indigenous identities, cultural practices and knowledge

digital divide—the gap between people who have access to digital technologies such as cell phones and internet and those who don't

digital literacy—the ability to find, evaluate and communicate information using digital technology

domesticity—relating to home and family life, such as running a household or raising a family

educational theories—ways of understanding education, including why learning is important and how the learning process works

etiquette—the rules and customs of what our society thinks is polite and acceptable behavior

extreme weather event—a time of unusually extreme weather of any kind, from heat waves to floods, that can have devastating impacts on people, animals and the environment; such events will increase as climate change worsens

fosterage—in the context of ancient Celtic culture, the raising of another family's child, based on a mutual agreement between allies

global citizens—people who understand that we are all citizens of the world and are all connected, and who take action to improve their communities and the world

heterosexual—romantically or sexually attracted to people of the opposite sex

human right—a basic right that every human is entitled to without discrimination, such as life, freedom of expression and education

land-based education—a form of education, also known as land-based learning, that is rooted in traditional Indigenous knowledge and involves learning from the land

nature schools—schools that philosophically value nature-based learning and where education takes place outdoors; also referred to as forest schools

philosophy—the study of questions about human life, including the concept of reality and human nature; the term comes from ancient Greece and means "love of wisdom"

portables—stand-alone movable buildings meant as a temporary solution to overcrowding in schools by creating additional classroom space

pronouns—in the context of gender, the words we use in the place of someone's name, such as *she*, *he*, and *they*; many people share their pronouns so that others know how to correctly refer to them

property taxes—money that people must pay to the government if they own land and/or a building; the money funds community services such as schools and libraries

race—any of the different groups people are often divided into based on physical characteristics considered common to people of shared ancestry, such as the color of their skin; it's important to note that race is an invented concept that has often been used to justify treating groups of people differently and unfairly

sustainable—in the context of being environmentally friendly, refers to a way of using resources that ensures there will be enough left for the future

truth and reconciliation—in Canada, the term refers to both a national commemorative day to honor and acknowledge the children who were sent to residential schools (those who survived and those who didn't), as well as a national commission created to expose the truth about residential schools and propose actions to help renew a relationship with Indigenous Peoples based on respect and cooperation

tuition—fees that must be paid to receive education; public schools typically do not charge tuition, but private schools and postsecondary intuitions typically do

unconstitutional—breaking the rules of a political system

undergraduate—refers to a student's first degree at a university (typically called a bachelor's degree)

RESOURCES

Print

Bridges, Ruby. *This Is Your Time*. Delacorte Press, 2020.

Camlot, Heather. *Secret Schools: True Stories of the Determination to Learn*. Owlkids, 2022.

Giannella, Valentina. *We Are All Greta: Be Inspired to Save the World*. Laurence King Publishing, 2019.

Hughes, Susan. *Off to Class: Incredible and Unusual Schools Around the World*. Owlkids, 2011.

Newman, Carey, and Kirstie Hudson. *The Witness Blanket: Truth, Art and Reconciliation*. Orca Book Publishers, 2022.

Polak, Monique. *Why Humans Work: How Jobs Shape Our Lives and Our World*. Orca Book Publishers, 2022.

Ruurs, Margriet. *School Days Around the World*. Kids Can Press, 2015.

Singh, Rina. *Grandmother School*. Orca Book Publishers, 2020.

Smith, Monique Gray. *Speaking Our Truth: A Journey of Reconciliation*. Orca Book Publishers, 2017.

Wilson, Janet. *Shannen and the Dream for a School*. Second Story Press, 2011.

Yousafzai, Malala, with Patricia McCormick. *I Am Malala: How One Girl Stood Up for Education and Changed the World*. Little, Brown Books for Young Readers, 2014.

Online

Britannica Kids: kids.britannica.com

The Canadian Encyclopedia: thecanadianencyclopedia.ca/en

CBC Kids News: cbc.ca/kidsnews

Kids Help Phone: kidshelpphone.ca

National Geographic Kids: kids.nationalgeographic.com

PFLAG: pflag.org; pflagcanada.ca

Time for Kids: timeforkids.com

UNICEF: unicef.org

The Witness Blanket: witnessblanket.ca

World History Encyclopedia: worldhistory.org

ACKNOWLEDGMENTS

First and foremost I would like to acknowledge that the lands upon which I live are the unceded Traditional Coast Salish Lands including the Squamish (Sḵwx̱wú7mesh), Tsleil-Waututh (səlilwətaɬ) and Musqueam (xʷməθkʷəy̓əm) Nations. Thank you to the people of these Nations for allowing me to live, raise my family, study and work here on these Lands.

When writing this book about school, I was keenly aware that the only reason I was able to do so is because of my own years of schooling. I am so grateful for my educational experience, and I also know how rare it truly is. Writing this book has been an emotional experience. As these pages explain, education has been very unequal through history—and still is today. Reading about these injustices is heartbreaking. All young people deserve to receive an education where they feel safe to be their wonderful, beautiful, complete selves. Together we can work to make this a reality.

Thank you to my incredible editors, Kirstie Hudson and Monique Polak, as well as to Orca Book Publishers for this opportunity. Thank you also to Elaine Su and Sarah Robertson-Barnes. Elaine offered invaluable insight and helped shape this book. Sarah acted as my wonderful expert reader. Both are inspiring, talented, hardworking women whom I deeply admire and am honored to call my friends.

Finally, thank you to my family. They have supported me in millions of ways, big and small. Thank you to my husband and parents for supporting me throughout the writing of this book, and through all of my goals. I am so grateful.

Thank you, everyone!

INDEX

*Page numbers in **bold** indicate an image caption.*

INDEX (CONTINUED)

NAME: JESSI
9/10
10/10
8/10
NAME: SHELDON
7/10
35
47
31
57

From the PAST to the PRESENT and into the FUTURE!

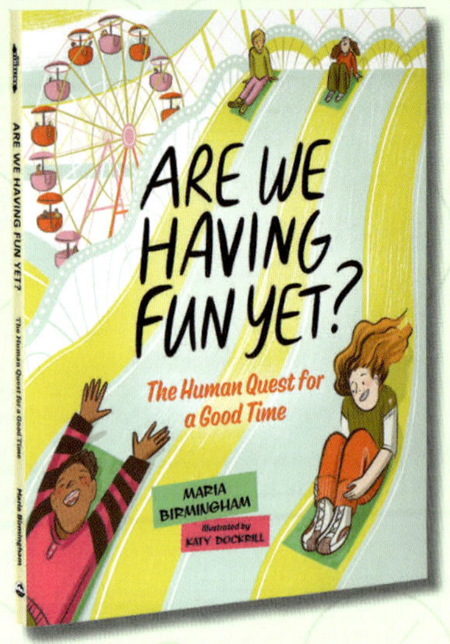

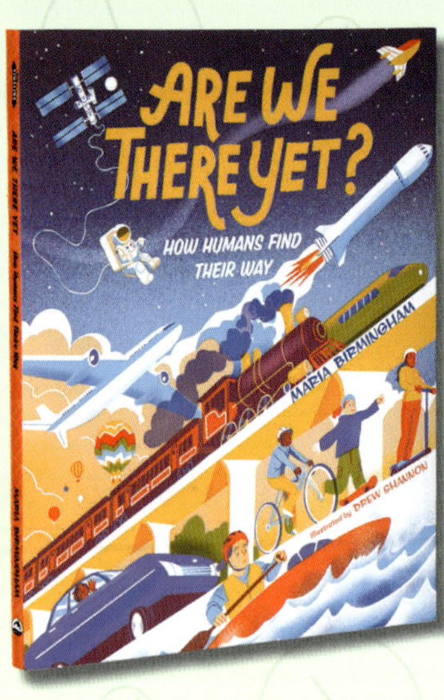

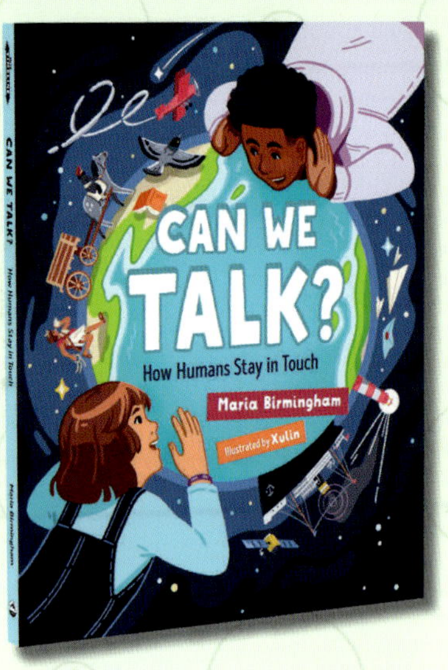

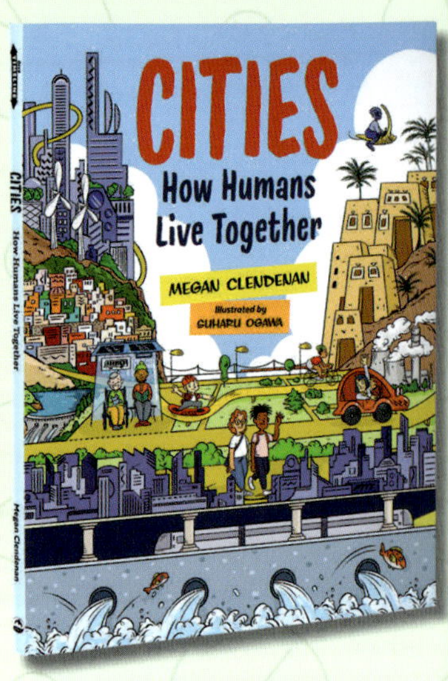

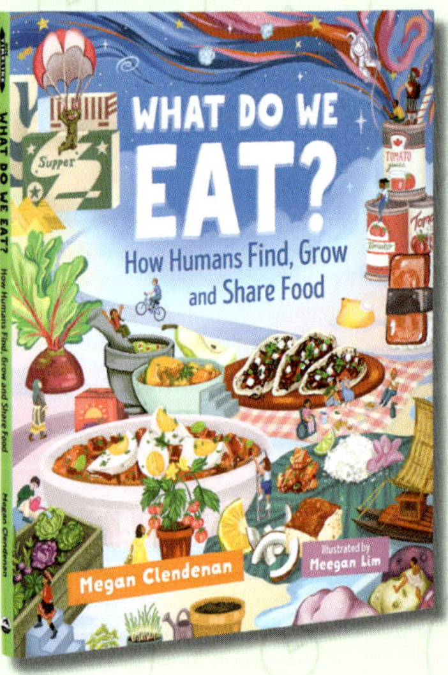

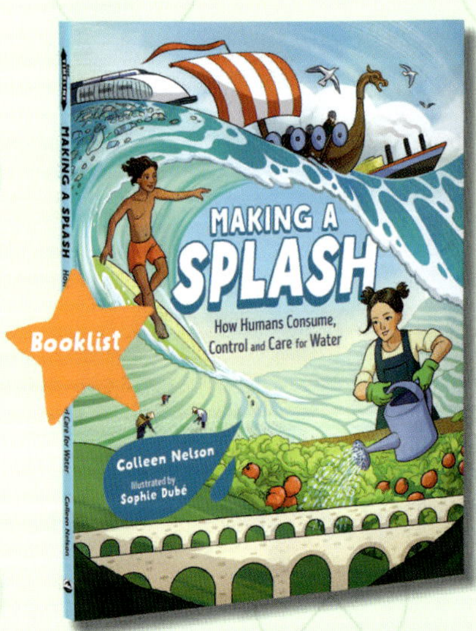

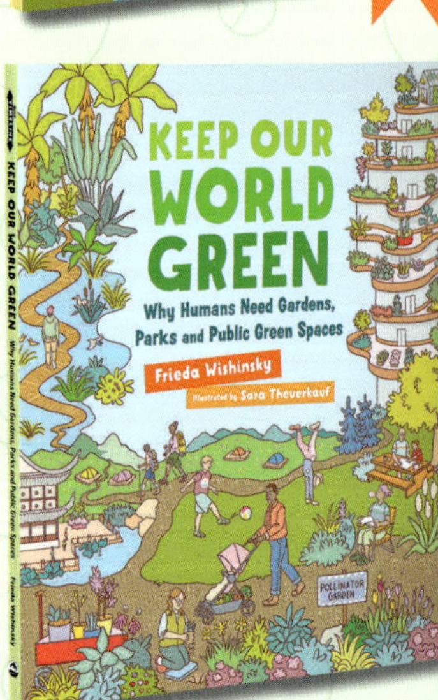

The Orca Timeline series explores how big ideas have shaped humanity. Discover what our collective history can tell us about the planet today and tomorrow.

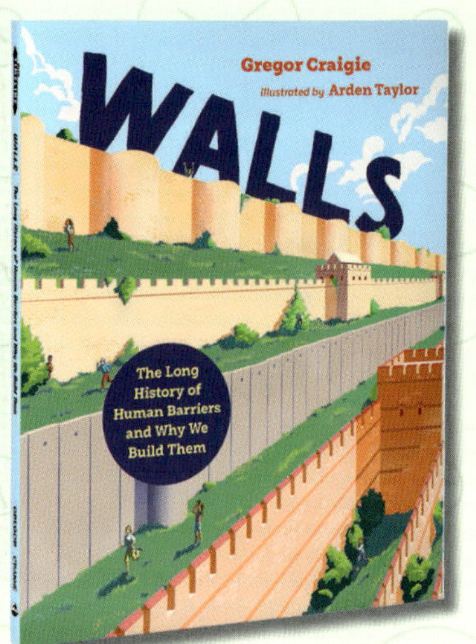

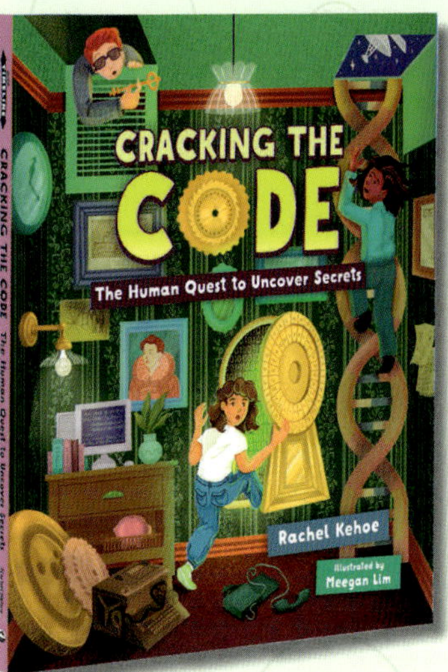

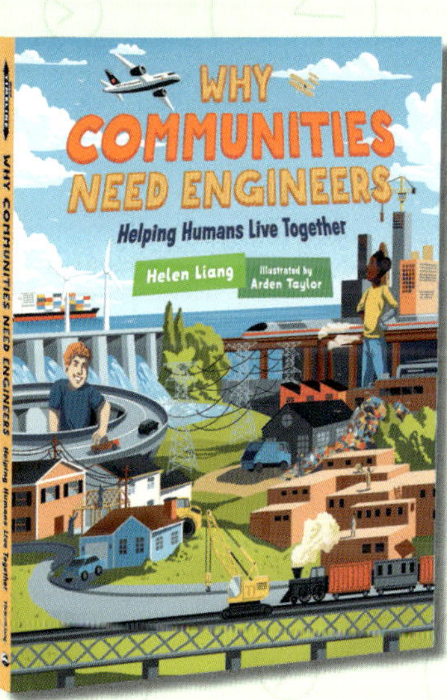

“These thorough and timely titles will make excellent additions to any library collection.”

—*Booklist*, starred review for the Orca Timeline series

NOTTING HILL PHOTOGRAPHY

LEAH PAYNE is a writer, editor, public librarian and mother. She holds a bachelor's degree in communication from Simon Fraser University and a master's degree in library and information studies (MLIS) from the University of British Columbia. Leah lives in British Columbia with her family. She loves reading and learning and would probably go to school forever if she could! Leah is also the author of *Less Is More* and *Get Outside!*, both published by Orca.

COURTESY OF PAIGE JUNG

PAIGE JUNG is a Chinese Canadian illustrator, muralist and artist from so-called "Vancouver," British Columbia. Using digital, gouache and acrylic mediums, Paige is known for her proficient use of color and gestural shapes to create illustrations that tell stories of connection, wonder, community and what makes us human. Paige is grateful to be creating, living and gathering on the unceded territories of the xʷməθkʷəy̓əm (Musqueam), Sḵwx̱wú7mesh (Squamish) and səlilwətaɬ (Tsleil-Waututh) Nations.

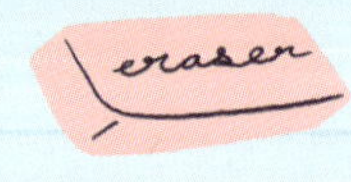